Jellyfish,

WHERE ARE YOU GOING?

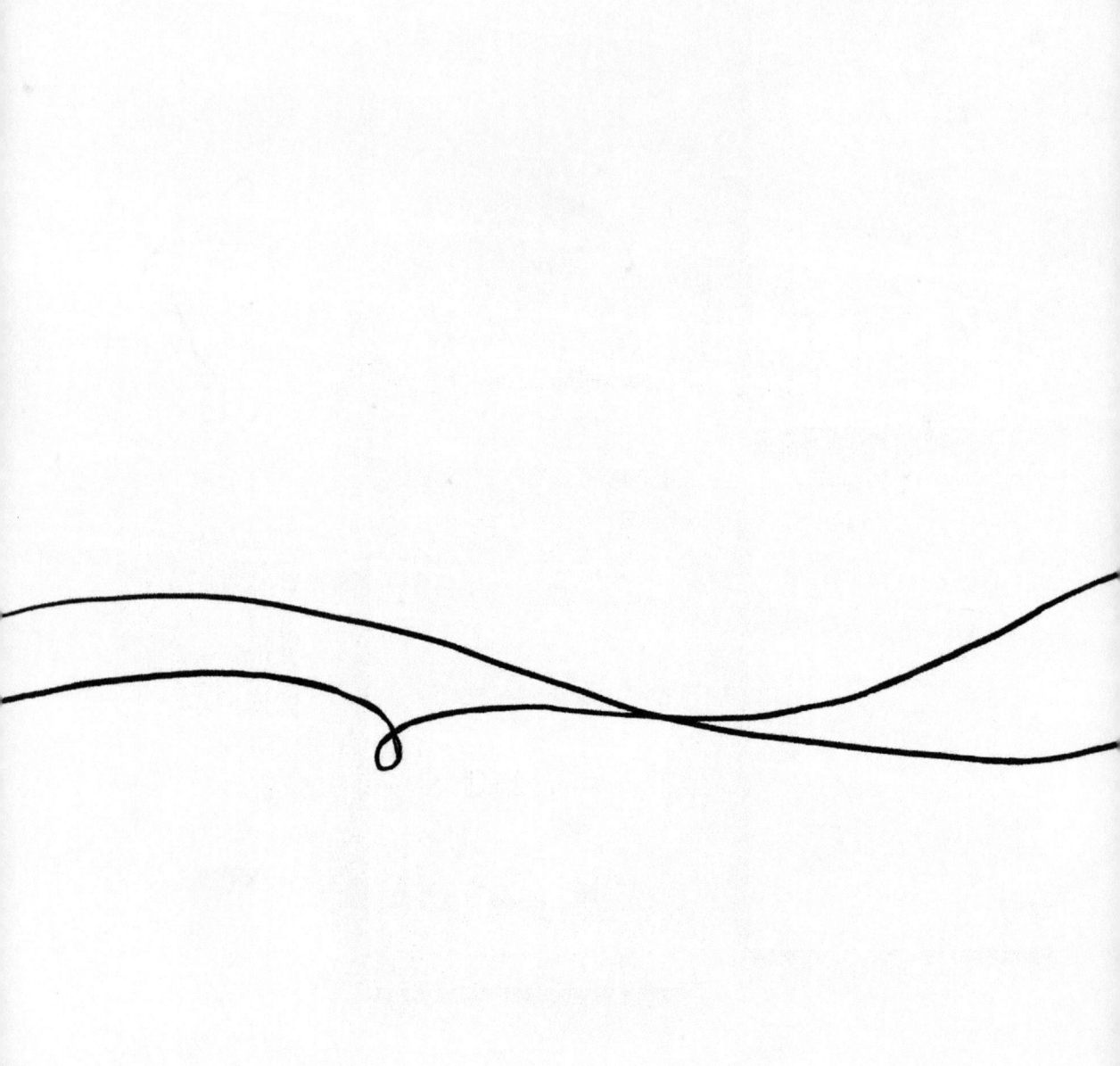

Want to **look inside?**
Scan this code!

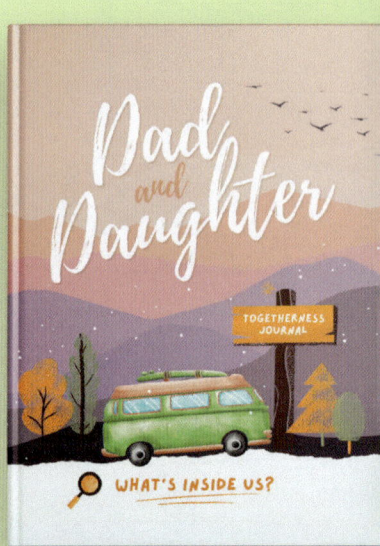
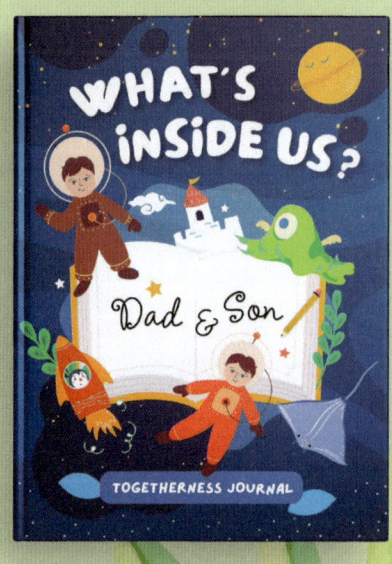
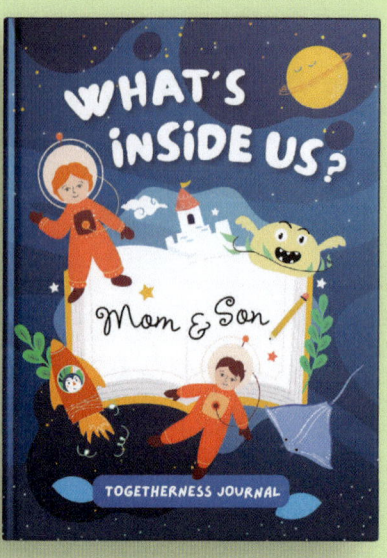
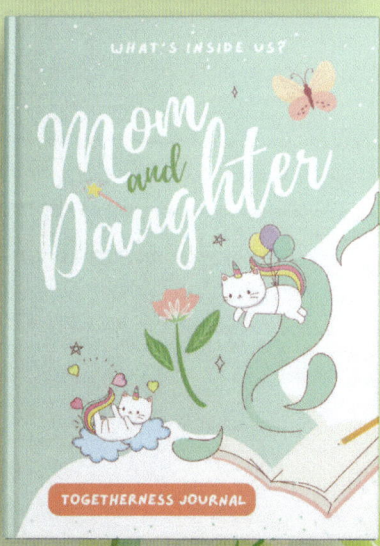

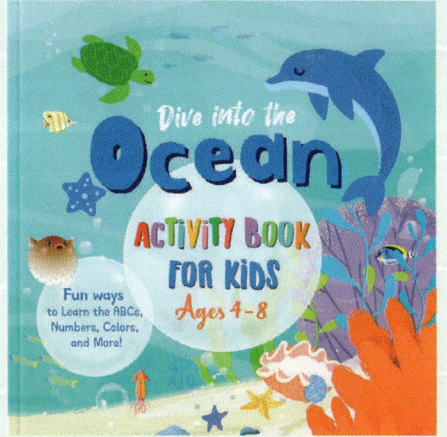
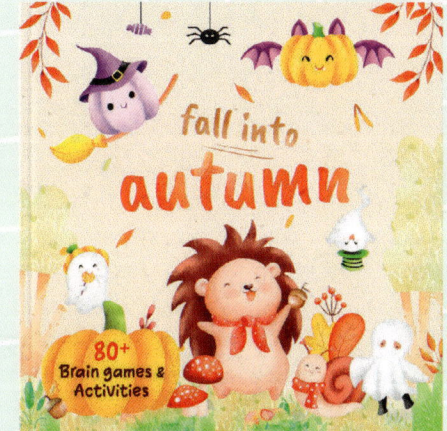
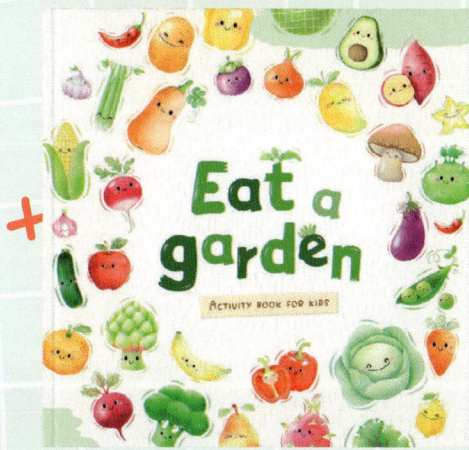
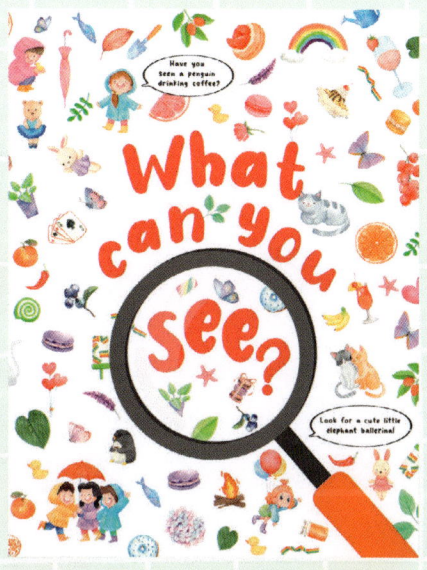
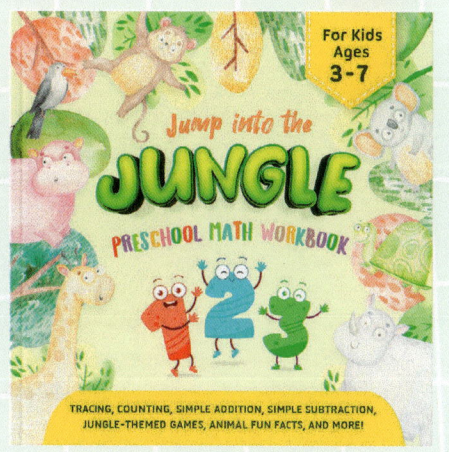

CHECK OUT OTHER TITLES AT
ENGAWABOOKS.COM

Bring Joy to your Kids
with 25 Drawing Activities

Scan this code to download a free copy

Members of Engawa Readers' Club, parents and teachers are welcome to download and print this file for personal, family or classroom use.

Printed in Great Britain
by Amazon